Three Doors, One Room

poems by

Tony Luebbermann

Finishing Line Press
Georgetown, Kentucky

… Three Doors, One Room

Copyright © 2022 by Tony Luebbermann
ISBN 978-1-64662-920-6 First Edition
All rights reserved under International and Pan-American Copyright Conventions. No part of this book may be reproduced in any manner whatsoever without written permission from the publisher, except in the case of brief quotations embodied in critical articles and reviews.

ACKNOWLEDGMENTS

The poems here are a testimony to the generosity of many who have taught me about poetry in Tucson's rich offering of classes and workshops. Their generosity is what shines in these poems; any tarnish is the result of idleness and incomplete polishing on my part. I give these unnamed friends and teachers my grateful thanks. I must also give credit to the dedicated staff of the University of Arizona Poetry Center which organizes and makes available every day the rich and varied resources of the Poetry Center's unique and outstanding collection of over 50,000 books of poetry. A library is known for its collection but without programming the collection is largely dormant. The Poetry Center's offerings of readings, classes, and special events and displays is gratefully noted here. I also note the exceptional teaching of the faculty of the Vermont College of Fine Arts where I received by MFA in poetry in 2010. Natasha Sajé, my first semester advisor at VCFA, has thankfully continued her advisory role and provided me with valuable comments about these poems. Her generosity and dedication are at the core of what poetry is about.

My thanks to Finishing Line Press for selecting *Three Doors, One Room*, for publication. And last, but certainly not least, I thank Susan, who remains the main reason why, yesterday, today, and tomorrow, I love to live.

Publisher: Leah Huete de Maines
Editor: Christen Kincaid
Cover Art: Tony Luebbermann
Author Photo: Susan Luebbermann
Cover Design: Elizabeth Maines McCleavy

Order online: www.finishinglinepress.com
also available on amazon.com

Author inquiries and mail orders:
Finishing Line Press
PO Box 1626
Georgetown, Kentucky 40324
USA

Table of Contents

First Words
Darwin's Islands 1
Blind Beyond Bending 2

First Door
Instant by Instant 4
Day Moon 5
Her Wondrous Voice 6
Completeness 7
Some Angels and Their Cities of Dust 8
How Raven Writes Poems 9
Trees and Stones Deep Speaking 10

Second Door
The Thimble Thief 12
The Wordkeeper's Dance 13
The Wheel 14
A Toast to the Language of International Economics 15
Intersection Song 16
Instructions for Finding Harmonious Sounds 17
The Plural of Die is Dice 18
Thrift Shop 19
Riddle 20

Both Doors Open
Desert Night Magic 22
Staking Claim 23
On Roses at Night Under Stars 24
Seesaw 25
Childhood 26
What We Know 27

The Third Door
Whale Falls 30
Winter 31
Blue 32
Elegy from an Archaeological Field School 33

Last Words
How is it 35
After Storm 36

First Words

"The really explicit phrase is doors of perception."
Marianne Faithfull

Darwin's Islands

He is bent over the scatter
looking for a pattern, peering
through the jeweler's loop
of his collecting, his journals, his mind,
their lenses stacked
on his forehead like small saucers.
    Observation always:
finches and wrens, then
mockingbirds.

Facts and more facts—
keys to synthesis, far sightedness.
Beaks, barks, tooth and feather,
islands' quick difference, one after another,
Kodachrome negatives, a slide show.
Time, a loaf of sliced bread.

And there, right at his feet,
in layer upon revealing layer,
the ladders of stark shadow,
their rungs of luminous debris—
the stiff puddles of sea lion pups,
stink of carcasses, grinning skulls,
bones of the dead before birth,
thin as bookmarks.

Blind Beyond Bending

My eyes understand
how a Great Blue climbs
from river's tall grass,
slowly lifting wide wings,
slowly walking on air,
                over trees, into sky,
wingsteps words whispering
hush hush   hush hush
and then, unseen,
           hummingbird's seizing
of air in a *blurring buzz*
       of many stepwords
hanging just there
in leafy vine's bright orange flower,
and dragon-fly's *flat zig-zag,*
water-hovering,
           wingwords, green glinting,
also unseen (maybe droning shadows),
and when alight
on twig or Lily pad,
the water trembles   for the eye
counts *four* (count them again), *four wings!*
(Only archangels have more…)

In this sunlit afternoon,
all steps disappear, become soundless,
         un-found and if found, un-sure for
*the I needs time to bend
(and more time to bind)
and for each thing time-bent
there are other things seen
that will not be bound—*

First Door

"Between every two pine trees there is a door leading to a new way of life."
John Muir

Instant by Instant

A bee,
on fire
with pollen,
stumbles
from the heat
of the morning glory
and walks bright air
to the next flower,
the next fire.

In deep swale
of late afternoon
thistles
grow velvet in thinning light
while yellow swallowtails
kindle shadows.

Leaning through meadows
evening trees rise
in the mouth of night,
to the breath of star-veils.

Against their dark trunks,
fireflies press petals of light,
and out of night's scrim,
in countless chorale,
insects sing
the bright
brief sweetness
of our lives.

Day Moon

The day moon's palest at the noon,
a lilac angel's pistol, gray, exquisite.
A threat of exit, a thin balloon,
A bullet hole of nightly visit.

Lilac angel's pistol, gray, exquisite,
hint of death without the yellow eye.
The bullet hole of night's bold visit,
she's determined not to hide.

The hint of death in palest eye,
a look reflected in the mirrored glass.
She's bold, determined not to hide
the memories of disquiet past.

She watches me from rippled glass—
so I worry—the lake-cried loon!
Like memories of disquiet past
the day moon's palest at the noon.

Her Wondrous Voice

In desert spring with nature's wonder of monsoon,
the lowly cacti, *mammalaria*, bloom
in tiny stars bright of pink, white and scarlet
among soaring ridges of the southwest desert.

Between the up and down crosshatch of spines,
each shows its fiery jewels from nature's mine,
each wears a handsome wreath—a tiny crown—
no larger than a baby's fist. The brown

of desert is transformed as nature turns
profane to sacred. The desert burns
with color—fire from water! Her voice
calls forth miracles—rejoice!

Completeness

      Before sun, the fold in lake-sky
tinted bright unsullied rose,
and   back
      from
  shore
      trees sil-hou-ette
and glow through flat black
          boughs of birch leaves.
Pine needles
scratch light with crisp black splatter; dark ragged
blueberry bushes boulder-the-ground.

Sky's trunk-dashed red rests
on lake's mirror line,
      horizon as time hesitates   intact
  (the day waits
                somewhere offshore)
with no motion to measure, no sound, then—
into sky—
     a million
grains of change
explode to day.

Some Angels and Their Cities of Dust

The Angels:

Pipevine, Orangetip,
Cloudless, Hairstreak,
Metalmark, Fritillary,
Brushfoot, Checkerspot,
Crescent and Buckeye,
Viceroy, Admiral,
Hackberry, Emperor,
Woodnymph and Satyr,
Monarch and Queen,
Two-tailed Swallowtail,
Skipper, Longtail,
Cloudgiving,
Skippering.

The Cities:

Verbena,
Lantana,
Salvia and Mint,
Sweetbush, Rabbitbush
Buckeye, Sweetwillow,
Mustard
        and Pea.

How Raven Writes Poems

Consider dinosaur at the mossy spring,
The massive shape, the wide-spaced feet
Shuffling slowly among stuttering ferns.
Its words are movements, steps placed

Then underlined by long heavy tail,
Leaving pool-words, phrases of bent bracken.
When spongy soil turns to bound loam,
On quarried slab is the dinosaur's sparse poem.

Now consider the raven's dark bent wing: purpled,
Glossy, burnished by rushing air and light,
A shining plow turning space and time,
Roiling wind into great waves. Each row,

Feather-formed, foams the parched white shore,
Line after surging line. Impossible shells
Placed there as glistening words, epic words,
Each set there by a whirling quill.

Trees and Stones Deep Speaking

With water, a stone may sigh for the language of stones
is naked, skin-written, rough, or smooth, spoken
without the means a tree has with leaves, and so,
articulates instead by bent water—bubbling and gurgle
for conversation, ripple, and eddy for soft laughter,
by waterfall, pride, and by glittering deep-run pools,
exuberance. Then, there is anger by flood.

In quiet moments stones speak by held light—
hold one in your hand, feel the warm eloquence.

The language of trees is murmurings, a rustling rise and fall
of words written by leaf or gleaming needles spoken green
by the wind as polysyllabic, simultaneous passages,
where entire histories are discussed in a single puff.
(The talk of all our centuries can pass an afternoon
among nodding branches of a tree.)

And when stilled in gold autumn light, their voice
is more than radiant: touch a leaf, see brilliance pain—
                countless tinctures in each leaf's verse.

With language, comes silence: air wheels smoke,
birds fall, fish bob belly-white against smutty stone.
Winter parses; words, snow-weighted, slow.

We hold bizarre pieties, our language for such states,
our disjoint grammars for water, air, fire, ice.
We have no cognates, no verbs to join,
but the babbling separation is ours, ours alone,
for deep kernels, ripe kernels thresh in the shouting
word-filled rain when each tree, each stone,
with each bright tear, speak and rejoin.

Second Door

"The beauty of the university consists not only of unity in variety, but also of variety in unity."
Umberto Eco

The Thimble Thief

Once she started she could not stop.
She found them left on shop counters
sometimes behind bric-a-brac,
once in a corner on a brown tile floor,
and once in the pocket of a greatcoat
hanging on the back of a door.
She took one that sat next to a bottle
of scotch and found another, in the morning,
on a frosted windowsill. And lying
by a silver candlestick was another
lined with soot. It blackened
the end of her nose. Then one fell
out of a horse's ass. It smelled like wind
and rain. And one loosely wrapped
in cellophane that cricked and creaked
on opening. And that same night
she found another made of brass,
tucked in the heavy bark of an oak.
And while washing her hands
just before bed one appeared
in a bar of lavender soap. Then
she saw one made of gold, floating in air,
held there, she supposed, by God's request—
so, she reached for it.

The Wordkeeper's Dance

She carries the hive on her back
walking a mauve landscape
passing pale hills, streams rocky with storm,
through meadows in thunder, and fields—
some darkly plowed, some barely sown,
misted with green or barren with stone.

She walks at the speed of a shade
that lengthens in late afternoon.
From the moving hive thoughts fly out
searching the woods for the verdict of words—
words that leaf dry limbs of desire
and stretch to touch the tortoises' fire.

They speak in return by a spherical dance
where steps must attend a shifting terrain.
If her steps are too slow words turn stale.
Too thick to fill combs, they crumble and spill.
If her steps are too fast words run thin
and drip the ground dark with shadow.

The Wheel

When I was a young man, living in town, unmarried,
without ambition, a carnival arrived with a song,
a song so alluring I rode its wheel, a great round
looming over our village, its spokes bright with blinking lights
dazzling every direction, its gondolas flashing circles,
a blur of color spinning night sky as it turned up
and around, and I saw the village turn small,
the streets narrow, lit by tiny ponds of light spaced
along sidewalks, saw people I probably knew
but did not recognize, move slowly as mere dots,
saw cars crawling like insects on a shelf, their headlights,
thin antennae sweeping back and forth turning
up and down streets, and the stores, Marvin's
Hardware, The Haunted Book, were all barely visible,
and at the top of this ride the wheel stopped,
and as the gondola gently rocked back and forth,
I was overcome by longing, such longing! — the breeze
bringing a fresh scent of sage from far beyond the village,
Orion's belt gleaming with strength in the night sky,
mountain tops beyond, fired by the sunset, turning magnetic
in their winged magnificence, their splendor untainted, alive—
and so strong the attraction, the magic of this high place
reaching deep into my well of yearning,
I vowed to leave the village,
vowed to strike out and beyond for a new life,
and then

the wheel moved, turned past this zenith, and started down
so the village with every stop and start loomed larger
and more familiar, and as the mountains, the stars,
and the scent of sage disappeared with the horizon,
a sadness overcame me, the people raised their faces and
waved, the storefronts became familiar, and I,
realizing I was without further destiny,
stepped off the wheel and never rode again.

A Toast to the Language of International Economics

The passages are dry as toast,
no emotional moisture, brittleness
loud with grind and crunch, crunch
and grind. Something needs to be added
to soften the stiffness of import licensing,
tariffs, exchange controls, reciprocity.
The constant phrase, "*It is notable that . . .*"
is the numbing aftertaste of this legalese.
Still, rigid surfaces support butter
and marmalade: cultural exchanges,
Kiwis donated to San Diego's zoo,
speeches extolling the virtues of freedom,
virtuous junkets of politicians pawned
to the click-flash of photographs by lobbyists.
Further still, in this non-perfect world,
mistakes are always made, and *it is notable that*
toast almost always lands jelly-side down
with its clean dry side hiding the messiness—
safe houses, informants, water boarding, renditions—
all the numbness so necessary for peace.

Intersection Song

Next to black smears on tire beaten curbs,
and cracked gutters filled with dead weeds
where muffled thumps of heavy metal song
beat to the thrum of idling cars,
where pigeons peck away
at a dark feathered mess mashed to the curb
like a shift of miners wielding picks,
in a scene of black windows, spewing bad air,
several cars back and a thousand feet down,
in a cross shaft of someone's claim
waiting for the red to turn green.

And in this mine of exhausted hearts,
of veins empty of all but fumes,
with the numbing blur of passing cars,
of shopping carts piled with junk filled bags,
and ragged men crossing nowhere streets,
we rake for loose rock on the back overhead,
against the mountain's granite stare—
our god of stone that never smiles—
and catch a glow from the traffic device,
the shinning aura of a caution light,
the small yellow bird in a little yellow cage.

Instructions for Finding Harmonious Sounds

Find the best sound that complements another.
Example: the sweep-sway of a weeping willow

and the wrinkled cracks of a freezing lake,
or hiss of steam from this oven baked

pie with a folded napkin, scraping knife.
Maybe, the gassy stomach of a well-lived life

with hymns from church steeples down the street
that beat time with a blinking sign, "Bill's Fine Meats!"

And with gutter trash that rattles snoring drunks,
perhaps those graffiti corners tattooed with punks,

and gold wheat fields that whisper for miles,
or cardboard homes, breaking glass, drug trials

with limos that purr on boxwood grounds.
Or complement the junkers rusting off Grand

with cigar smoke and the ice cube clink of single malt scotch.
Then, paper bagged beers and relit butts (puff! puff!)

match the sparkling windows of Tif's and Sak's.
And the florescent buzz from a Circle K

with the clicks of shiny nails and cultured pearls,
and grubby red hands swilling bent pails

can sound like sequined poodles chewing steak.
So, try mangy dogs that growl the dark streets

with this CEO's golden parachute (pop!),
or this PayDay loan that opens for 40% (ugh!)

with a chatty socialite (she is so cute!).
But be sure to try the rank, dank, stink of rotting fruit
with the soundless lives of the always mute.

The Plural of Die is Dice

Ever wonder about random events?
Like slicing butter over hot rice,
a song of notes that slide and melts.
Or think of all the things you wrote
in yesterday's journal: about
your sister's latest style, the way
she underlines, dots I's . . . *a heart?*
And what she says about her friends!
That Cary's making out with Jim
and Sarah's uncertain of her new beau Dill.
But there's jobs to be had . . . and wealth.

So there's Land's End and Chico,
Wall Street and Halliburton, then
Bass and IBM. The babies come
and all gets serious. At Haley's Comet
the beer is warm, an overstuffed chair
is used for music. And so: life insurance,
or not. Perhaps a summer home on Lake
Perwagun, a trip to Italy. Some rain.

You hand a sunrise to your sister.
The parents die. Inheritance:
the house, the cars, the yard sale.
And in a while cancer sings to her breasts,
hums at your testicles and liver.
Still, the kids go to college? Maybe travel,
perhaps get jobs? No suicides yet.

The coffins continue to blossom.
The telephone rings. You whistle
a tune that tastes of sand,
pick a feather off the ground,
fold a yellow beach towel twice.
Put it away.
Listen to a wail on the radio.
Buy a grave.

Thrift Shop

Side by side, black leathers scuffed,
A right and left shoe lie in rest.
These worn soles grace, from heel to welt,
Hard sung tunes: the deep scarred blues
Of smoky bars, the sound of tough
Low words spit out, pissing bad news,

And cursing the seven-point spread taken
By those standing, arms raised, fists
Clenched, cheering at a halfback's first
Score in their favor. One warm beer
Later, a new face on fate's token,
Then others pound backs, sloppily cheer.

I find these scenes on thrift shop's shelves:
Shirts faded, folded like shouts, cuffs,
Hoarse-frayed, yellow stained from hard efforts,
Dog-eared collars, shoes stained by spit.
Here, wear shines thin on pants and shirts
From hard walk of work or the hard lack of it.

Searching these narrow aisles, the racks
Strewn with others' discarded garb,
I sort through musty heaps to grab
Something that will lighten a hard day's
Burden from my aching back,
For the chance luck will turn and pay odds…

Maybe these shoes: their laced-up fate
Can't be worth much—only a buck,
Or less. And wealth does walk to luck
(Maybe a hundred-dollar bill she's
Slipped inside that insole's gap!)
    For hope shines last on our old shoes.

Riddle

Most ardent for life of all our discovered kin,
third cousin to a single grain from fiery fields of sun,
twig dipped in the pride of Prometheus, wing-
feathered with smoke and flame, the flare of its strike-
light shatters dark like a bell struck. God's trickster,

tool riven by a tyranny of pain, we are cursed to guard
its dazzle, its wrathwreath, its smoking sulfured head
crowned from the birth of the universe, its hovering hosts
moving without caution, moving through voracious rebirth;
an appetite of hot vomit, it spits *uncare*, turns skin

raw with screams, cinders worlds, but *is* winterwarm.
Subject of fear but also embraced, hot twin
to our opposed thumb, it breathes what we breathe,
and holds at ready our sulfurous second tongue.

Both Doors Open

*"People don't know how to make a leaf,
but they know how to destroy one."*
Hope Jahreb, Lab Girl

*"A real man knows how to nurture nature
and nurture himself from nature."*
Marcus L. Lukusa

Desert Night Magic

Sometimes I stand in moon-shadow,
saguaro's spell brushing my skin,
the desert spewing its dark perfume,
the sky, the air, charmed with light,
listening to the cast of spells nearby:
the bright shrill of hawk's *pee-nt,*
the arroyo's deep *who whos* of owls,
the bright thin *yips* of coyote covens,
while watching the bats weave stars,
        and trying to twig the magic,
        to learn the incantations
how dawn makes night disappear
without pain, and marveling—
        with only a wave of twilight's wand—
its enchanted return.

Staking Claim

I earned my claim here today
by long bushwhack and sweat
through rough terrain
and hours of look and listen.

On the lake a loon shivers its image,
lifts it cry across granite and leaves,
winds rise and brush away, sighing again and again.
Mirrored light of a redding sun tints the trees,
darkness begins to rise, pine needles drift down
to the lake's shadow, fall of a late summer day
sharpens the edge of the changing season,
and my place as the first person here.

I rise to go, and step to an old pine to pee,
to seal the bark wet with my claim.
But there in the tree before me
        the rusted head of a nail.

On Roses at Night Under Stars

With night sounds ticking and stars
bright staked to black, the fragrance
of roses blocked by heavy hedge
wafts from a neighbor's yard, across
property lines, fences, zoning, deeds
and covenants—a vitality ignoring restrictions,
penetrating through briar, vine and wood,
prevailing over laws, rules, morality,
artifact and judgment, bringing
the dark pulse of essential red, vivid,
more real in this night than day,
bringing scentlight woven into darklight.

Above, the stars, our witness trees of space
marking corners of our myths, our ancient
properties—Orion, Cassiopeia, Big Dipper,
Pole Star—shooting beyond us in breathless
cold transits, indifferent to human styles,
human forms, brought by time's tireless
shuttle weaving into the night the fire
from stars living, stars dead, fabric
at once holding both, opaque, mysterious
untouchable, chilling the uplifted face.

Seesaw

> *I've seen a Dying Eye...*
> —Emily Dickinson

Sitting in a chair with my back
to the east window as night comes,
the evening newspaper spreads colors
of the world across my lap.
To the west the news seems glorious.

                Suddenly,
a solid thump—something dropped—
and I look back over my shoulder
to see small feathers lit by the setting sun,
floating like embers from a kicked fire,
and, shining on the windowpane,
the imprint of a dove in flight,
feathers outstretched, each caught
in ghostly luminous dust. Even
its beak is there and the small left eye,
a dusty circle staring through the glass,
trying to see what it was it saw.

Childhood

In the middle of a wooded path, damp
from recent rain, a moose has stepped
in the leafy softness. I squat to look.
A big bull and each half of his deep track
weeps water—he is close, very close.
The tracks curve down the path
out of sight.

Shrieks of warning day and night
thunder the trestle above our swimming hole,
where on a humid summer day, insects
humming high, I press my ear to a train's rail
like an Indian scout in cowboy movies,
insulating the hot steel with my beach towel,
the tracks stretching across the trestle curving
away on the other side, listening for any
vibration of an approaching train. Hearing
none, I start across, picking my way hurriedly,
barefooted, in bathing suit, arms extended,
beach towel slung over my shoulder,
high above trees, the river below
glistening thin between the shinning rails,
the ties rough, hot, smelling of creosote,
and then, from around the curve, out of sight,
a whistle screams and at my feet the engine's
heavy throb.

I stand, peer down the path
and see nothing. I listen and hear nothing.
The path ahead waits, tense, alive. Pooled
with light, the track at my feet wrinkles
then shivers. The trestle trees around me
darken. The sky shakes and rumbles.

What We Know

The sun's needles lift,
tugging the cloth of earth to a gentle pause,
gathering in loose folds
       waves collected from night's shores,
            leaf breezes swirled into corners,
      clouds pressed vivid on dawn.

Along a log, hunting shrews hunted,
       fall into Mason jar traps, then weighed,
measured, released. Microscopes backdropped by white coats
of scientists, expand our sight, but
      in other settings
              deer antlers spring
     headless out of walls,
glowing candelabras of interwoven tusks
shadow boiling shark fins, the mat of hair horns,
weave of incantation's song, fumes of vat dyes.

Across bristly mirrored faces,
 the ritual morning strokes
       of soapy badger fur. Throughout the day
other echoes of spilled dust rub rough.
Corrosive winds enormously invisible.
The human tide carries only three things:
      belief,   hope,   or their pretension.

At a crossing we wait. Hundreds
       of railroad cars filled with sand travel
            from a now depleted shore, and

on mahogany tables delicate ivory frames display
pastel-colored shells, small and perfect,
    made rare
    by setting fire
            to entire keys.

Indifference to wellbeing, our wells go dry.

Viruses move
          in a mineral present.

And time as agent of change is everywhere raw,
        oozing and sore,

unpredictable winds move grains of sand, fresh blood
        dries black,
trees fall, maggots suck flesh,
                rot continues to rot.

Pulsing daylight pales the moon's face.
Along the beach crow calls rasp air.

Standing on sand,
        among broken shells,
our silhouettes grow faint.

The Third Door

"...*death transforms life into a destiny*..."
Simone de Beauvoir

Whale Falls

When a whale dies
       it sinks slowly
leaving a trail of streaming bubbles
          swarming upward
as water's great weight
gathering against the whale's falling body
presses harder and harder closing the spaces within,
its great length tumbling slowly down,
       through thousands of feet,
       then miles,
          falling   and   falling,
sometimes rolling gently over and over,
sometimes tumbling slowly end   over   end
  through cold crossing currents,
    through intersecting zones of temperature and life,
      through darting schools of jittery fish, shivering the light,
layer upon layer,   falling
in brightness,   then half-bright, then dust-light
until the whale is falling in dark,
and in this long fall
 the whale is accompanied by the deep songs of live whales
        singing out of the distance until
          landing on the sea's bottom,
raising a soft spray of dusty silt,
when songs stop and
the whale body settles and stills.

In the extreme cold of centuries
these decaying hulks, tons of flesh and bone,
        decompose slowly
microbes and bacteria,
       erode particle by particle, then
carried by currents traveling into vastness.

Like shipwrecks, these great hulks
are discovered on rare occasions
by remote sensors exploring the bottom of the sea and
are known as whale falls,
an event never witnessed, only inferred,
an event of human imagination.

Winter

Late at night in the desert cold,
birds settle on a chimney's edge
seeking warmth from the hearth below
where coals once cherry bright,
now dulled to gray, are heaped
against the iron fireback.

And sometimes when numbers
glowing on my bedside clock are small,
the dark erupts with feathered cries
from deep in the chimney's throat,
the desperate alarm of wild wings
thrashing on the black smoke shelf,
muffled by smothering soot—

                                        Each bout
of frantic thrumming shakes me awake,
but as they weaken and silences lengthen,
I sleep, unsettled, dreaming of a winter lake,
evergreens overhanging black ice,
a moonlit canopy where deer dance
on unsteady legs, hoofs chattering the ice,
front legs raised, waving, grasping air,

necks stretched, straining,
mouths reaching up,
up to branches and life
while the ice glows
 against the dark shore.

Blue

> *To comprehend a nectar*
> *Requires the sorest need.*
> — Emily Dickinson

There is little to say about dry chicken bones
except that their splinters are hard and sharp
and how these make such a painful connection
to the harsh retching sounds of a dog's struggle
as he opens and closes his mouth.

And because of blue I understand better
the import of foregrounding clouds,
how grey can shape and flatten the infinite,
and shadow the clearness we hold.
But in each of these moments
of darkness, despair, there is always
the closeness of promise and hope

as when I saw in my love's dark eyes
that moment of shimmer,
the intimate luminance that brushes the heart
the way birds flying dawn will sketch the sky,
a completeness that radiates in colors and form
for a picture more brilliant that light.

All from a kitchen floor canvas,
and a brush of red splintered bones.

Elegy from an Archaeological Field School

Grasshopper Pueblo, c.1300 AD,
Cibecue, Arizona

They lived hard, high
on the Mogollon Rim among dark pines.
They painted pottery in polychromes
of red and white, finely shaped,
and planted corn in spring soil cool after rain.

                                              Shells
from salt seas adorned their arms,
and, from the tropics, bright feathered
parrots perched in their homes.

Often, mothers young with newborns
buried on their chests, their rib bones
woven with the baby's—a basket
of mother and child cloistered in bone song.

Often too, children under ten
buried in graves empty of offerings,
empty of the pueblo's grieving
                                        for death
close to birth was further from love:
two large pottery shards used
to scrape a fetus from a dirt floor
uncovered in a garbage pit.
Between the shards, tiny notes
of their song—like those from a small bird.

Last Words…

How is it

                that a dog barks
seems happy about it

that fish   sew watery quilts
       in patterns that glitter
while embroidered above   are
      butterflies   gulls

that sunlight   in a waltz called wind
   laces leaves   so   freely

that rain   tats notes   of grace
     to clover   each blade
  each leaf

that waves   so smoothly   wave
              over seaweed currents
        under so much   blue

while geese   cross-stitch   the sky
       with cries   so raucous

that ants weave quickly
  through thick   wefts of grass

while we

knot our days   with bluster
slog pathless
     and stumble

on the glorious   cloaks of dawn

that could and should
             adorn us.

After Storm

Wind's sharp scissors slow my morning walk. At
My feet, autumn's leaf, red and so formed
It holds rain fresh from last night's angry talk
Of threaded fire, dark felt, thick sound. That storm

Tore mountain stones, cut trees, and stitched the air
So early morning forms a cold-hard sheath,
Dulling the light but lifting the dark. There,
Amid rough roots, out of the wind, I see

Pinned in this leafy cup a dying moth—
Its heart-wings beat in silent, helpless rings.
Black clouds sweep. In the east, a golden cloth
Unfurls to glorify these small frail things.
From high, the raucous blessing of the weaving geese
A song that shrouds this death,
                              every death, with earth's belief.

www.ingramcontent.com/pod-product-compliance
Lightning Source LLC
LaVergne TN
LVHW041558070426
835507LV00011B/1168